LET'S-READ-AND-FIND-OUT BOOK CLUB EDITION.

SALT

By AUGUSTA GOLDIN
Illustrated by ROBERT GALSTER

Thomas Y. Crowell Company • New York

Every day you use salt. You cannot live without it.

You need salt every day, yet it is not a food. Salt is a *mineral.*

A chemist calls salt *sodium chloride.*

You call it salt, or table salt.

Shake some salt into your hand. It feels dry and gritty.

Use your magnifying glass for a closer look. You will see broken grains of salt and crushed grains of salt. You will see salt grains stuck together in clumps.

You will also see perfect grains of salt. They look like this.

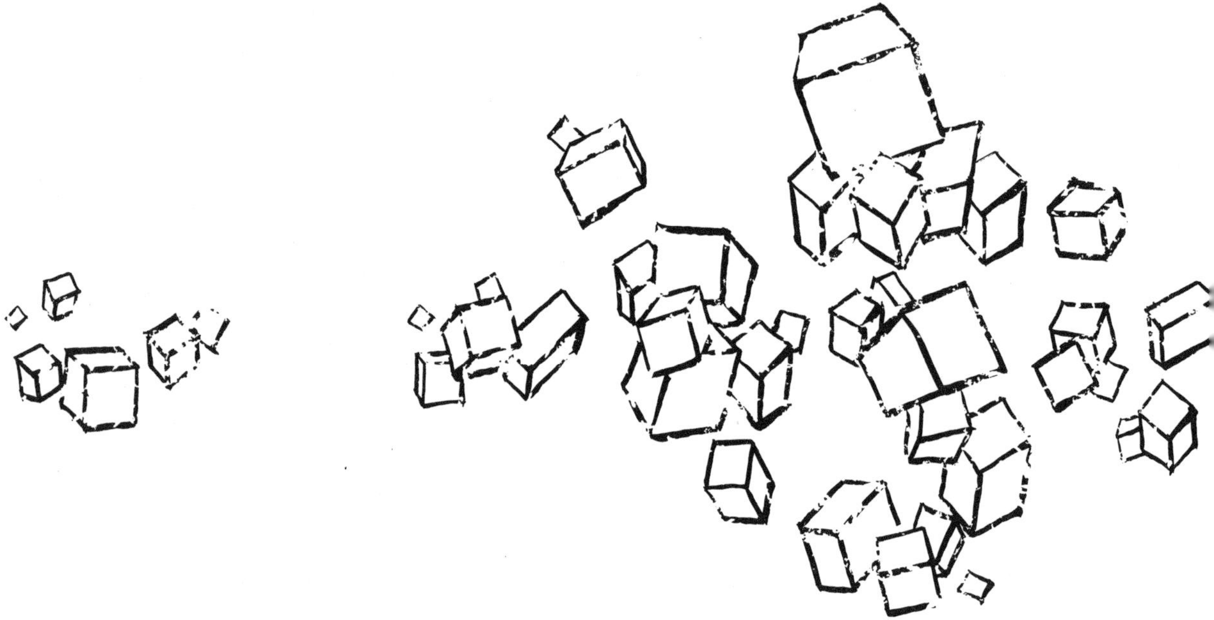

Each grain of salt is a little cube with six square sides.
The cubes are called salt *crystals*.
You can grow your own salt crystals on a string.

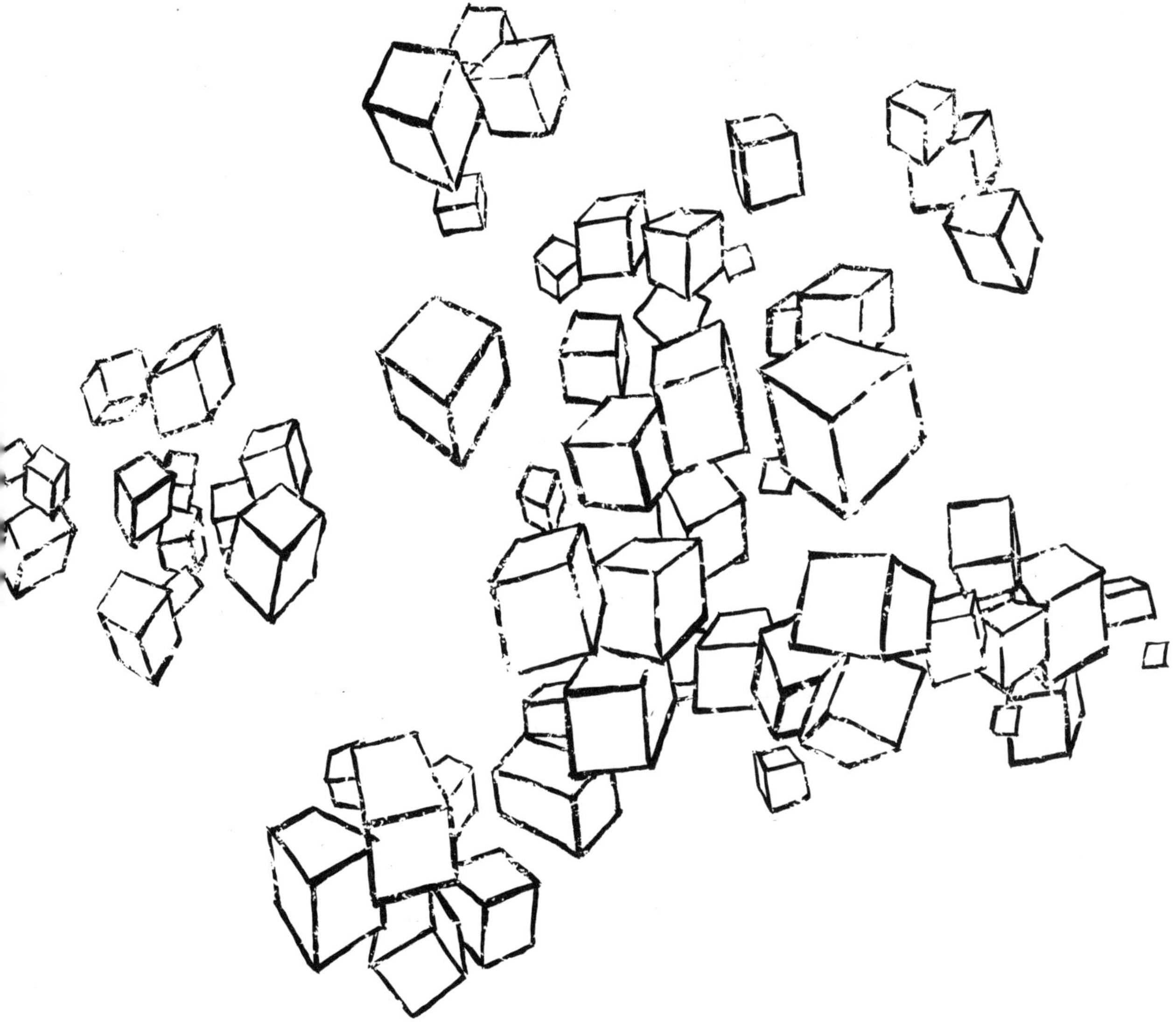

First you must make a salt solution by adding salt to water. Pour four tablespoonfuls of salt into a cup of warm water. Watch the salt crystals drift through the water.

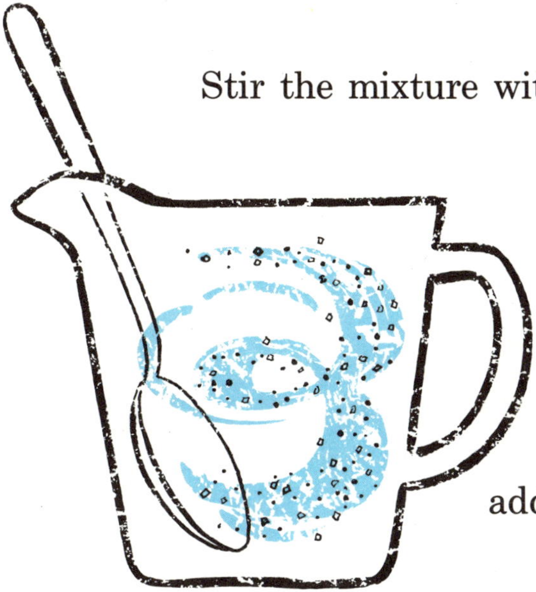

Stir the mixture with a spoon.

When the salt dissolves,
add one more tablespoonful of salt.

This time all the salt will not dissolve.
Some will settle on the bottom.

It is called *brine*.

Now you have a very strong salt solution.

To grow salt crystals on a string, you will need a glass, a pencil, a piece of fine string or thread, and a button. Fill the glass half full with brine. Tie the string to the pencil. Tie the button to the end of the string to hold it down. Lay the pencil across the top of the glass so the button hangs down into the brine. Put the glass in a place where it won't be moved. Don't move the string. Just look at it.

After four or five days you will have a salt string.

The part of the string that was out of the water will be crowded with salt. The salt was left behind when the water evaporated. There will be salt on the glass, too.

On the string below the water there will be crystals of salt.

You can grow crystals faster if you put a stick into a glassful of brine. Crystals will grow on the stick in two or three days, but they won't be as large as the crystals on the string. It takes time for large crystals to grow.

Some of the salt crystals on the string and the stick will be perfect. Use your magnifying glass to see them. A perfect crystal of salt has six sides.

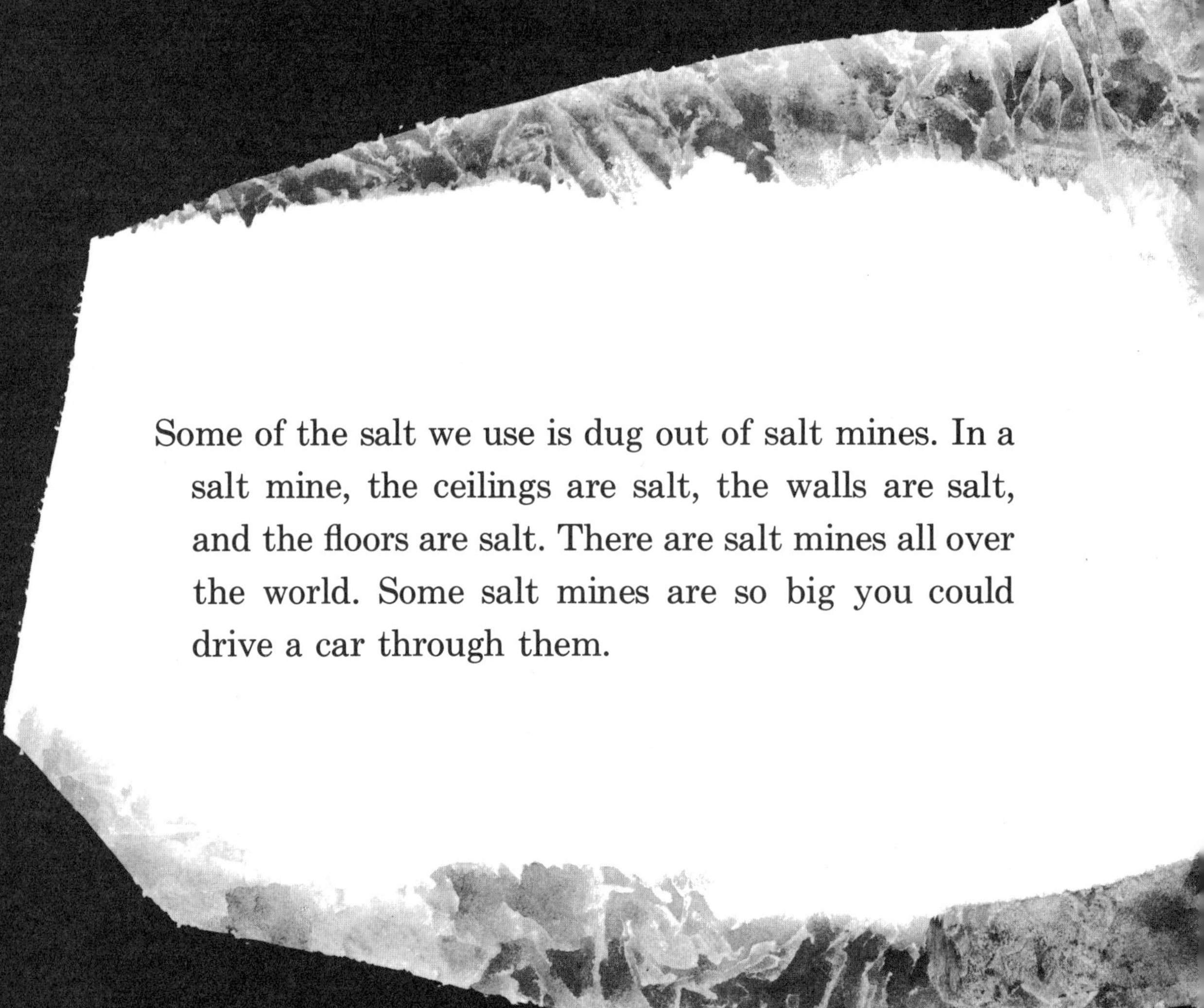

Some of the salt we use is dug out of salt mines. In a salt mine, the ceilings are salt, the walls are salt, and the floors are salt. There are salt mines all over the world. Some salt mines are so big you could drive a car through them.

The salt that you use may have come from a salt mine.

It may have come from a lake of salt under the ground.

It may have come from the salty sea.

Whether salt comes from mines, from underground lakes, or from the sea, first it comes from rocks.

All rocks have a little salt in them. Rainwater seeping through the ground dissolves some of the salt. Brooks, rivers, and underground streams carry this salt to springs and wells, to lakes and seas. Springs, wells, and lakes that have no outlct to the sea get saltier and saltier.

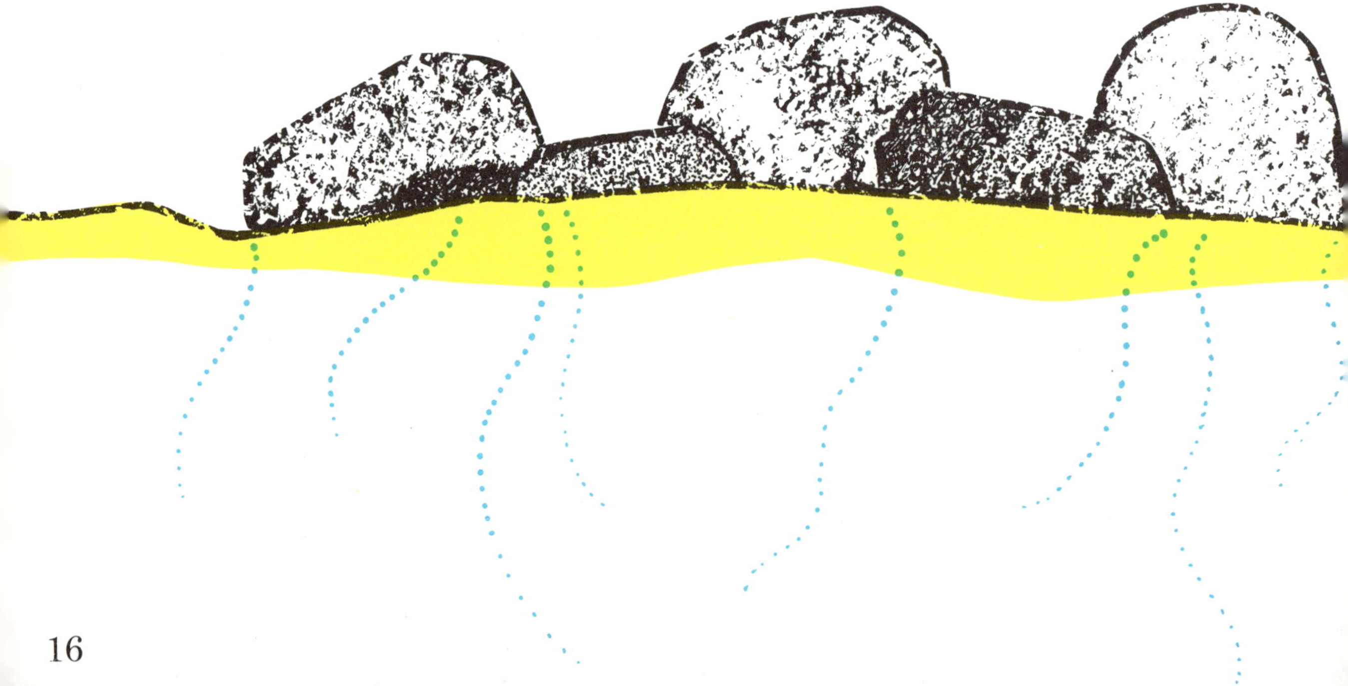

When the waters of a salty lake or ocean evaporate into the air, the salt does not evaporate. You can see the white lines of salt crystals where waves have splashed and dried on rocks. The water evaporates. The salt is left behind.

Sometimes all the waters of a salty lake evaporate into the air. Great beds of salt are left behind.

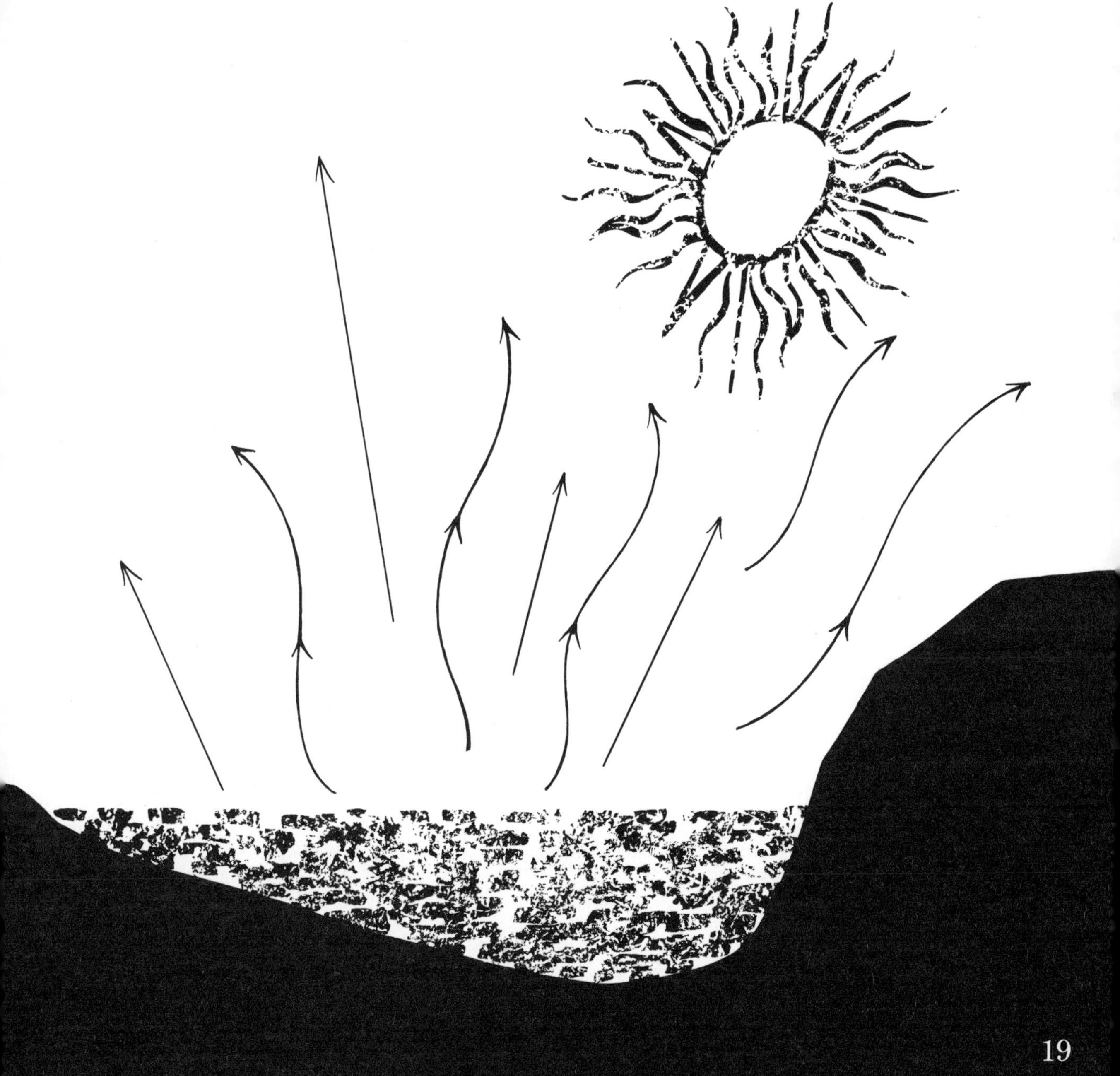

No matter where the salt comes from it can be used only when it is in solution.

Put a salt crystal on your tongue and see what happens.

The salt dissolves on your wet tongue. As soon as it dissolves you taste the salt. You have made a salt solution in your mouth. If your tongue were dry, the salt would not dissolve. You would not be able to taste the dry salt. Salt must be in solution before you can taste it.

There are many kinds of salt solutions inside your own body.

Next time you cry, taste your tears. They are salty.

Next time you perspire, taste the sweat. It is salty, too.

Blood is salty. Tears, sweat, and blood taste salty because they contain salt in solution.

Some salt solutions are weak. Some are strong and briny.
Brine is used to preserve food.

Codfish and herring are preserved with salt.

Cucumbers are put into salt brine to make pickles.

Salt is pounded with cabbage to make sauerkraut.

Meat is put into brine to preserve it.

Salt preserves food because bacteria that spoil food cannot grow in brine.

Salt is a mineral that is full of surprises.
You can stir it in water until it dissolves. The salt disappears.

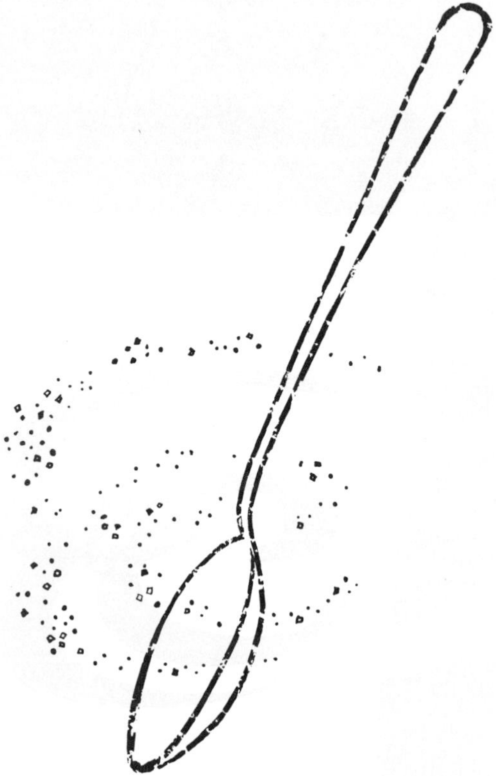

You can make it reappear out of the solution.
When the water evaporates the salt reappears.

You can do this a hundred times with the same cupful of salt.

But when you need salt you don't have to make salt solutions. You don't have to grow salt crystals. You find them ready-made all over the world.

Salt crystals are found in salt beds, and in salt mines deep under the ground. Salt lakes and deep salt wells are salt solutions. The ocean is the biggest salt solution of all.

ABOUT THE AUTHOR

AUGUSTA GOLDIN was born in New York City but grew up on a farm in the Catskill Mountains near Ellenville, New York. She was graduated from Hunter College, received a Master of Science degree from the City University of New York, and a doctorate of education from Teachers College, Columbia University.

Mrs. Goldin has worked on the staffs of several education publications and is the principal of a school on Staten Island, New York.

She has traveled around the world and visited Mexico, Canada, and Europe many times. She and her husband live on Staten Island. They have a daughter and a son.

ABOUT THE ILLUSTRATOR

ROBERT GALSTER has illustrated many books, designed book jackets and record-album covers, and painted murals. He is also well known for his Broadway theater poster designs, and in his spare time he is a map collector and has been for many years.

Born in Illinois, Mr. Galster grew up in Ohio and now lives in New York City.